GOS SWVES I

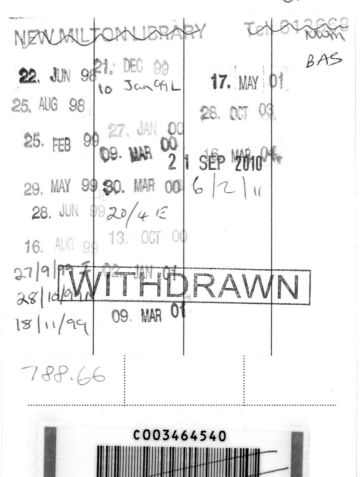

SWest.

Saxmania!
PopGreats/2.

Wise Publications
London/New York/Paris/Sydney/Copenhagen/Madrid

Exclusive Distributors:
Music Sales Limited
8/9 Frith Street,
London W1V 5TZ, England.
Music Sales Pty Limited
120 Rothschild Avenue,
Rosebery, NSW 2018,
Australia.

Order No. AM91547
ISBN 0-7119-3774-5
This book © Copyright 1994 by Wise Publications

Compiled by Peter Evans
Music arranged by Steve Tayton
Music processed by Ternary Graphics

Book design by Studio Twenty, London
Cover photograph by Julian Hawkins

Printed in the United Kingdom by
Halstan & Co. Ltd., Amersham, Bucks.

Your Guarantee of Quality
As publishers, we strive to produce every book
to the highest commercial standards.
The music has been freshly engraved and the book has been
carefully designed to minimise awkward page turns and to
make playing from it a real pleasure.
Particular care has been given to specifying acid-free,
neutral-sized paper which has not been chlorine bleached
but produced with special regard for the environment.
Throughout, the printing and binding have been planned to ensure
a sturdy, attractive publication which should give years of enjoyment.
If your copy fails to meet our high standards, please
inform us and we will gladly replace it.

Music Sales' complete catalogue lists thousands of titles and is free from
your local music shop, or direct from Music Sales Limited.
Please send a cheque/postal order for £1.50 for postage to: Music Sales Limited,
Newmarket Road, Bury St. Edmunds, Suffolk IP33 3YB.

And just look at some of the other
music you can play with Saxmania!…

Saxmania! Standards
Includes 'Catch A Falling Star'…
'As Time Goes By'…'Pennies From Heaven'…
and 31 more golden favourites.
Order No.AM78262

Saxmania! Jazz Hits
Includes 'Mood Indigo'…
'Take The 'A' Train'…'Take Five'…
and two dozen more all-time greats.
Order No.AM78254

Saxmania! Pop Greats
Includes 'Sailing'…'Stand By Me'…
'Nothing's Gonna Change My Love For You'…
and 29 more chart hits.
Order No.AM78247

Saxmania! Jazz Classics
Includes 'On The Sunny Side Of The Street'…
'Walking Shoes'…'Cute'…and 30 other jazz classics.
Order No.AM90100

Saxmania! Rock Hits
Includes 'Addicted To Love'…'Layla'…'Roxanne'…
and 20 other rock classics.
Order No.AM90101

Saxmania! Blues Greats
Includes 'Basin Street Blues'…
'Georgia On My Mind'…'Lazy Bones'…
and over 30 other essential blues numbers.
Order No.AM90099

Saxmania! Beatles Classics
Includes 'Eleanor Rigby'…'Hey Jude'…
'Yesterday'…and 32 other famous Beatles hits.
Order No.N090462

Saxmania! Big Band
Includes 'A Taste Of Honey'…'Night Train'…
'Opus One'…and 33 other Big Band numbers.
Order No.AM90122

Saxmania! Great Solos
Includes 'Baker Street'…
'Careless Whisper'…'Lily Was Here'…
'Your Latest Trick'…and nine more stunning solos.
Order No. AM90123

Another Day In Paradise

Words & Music Phil Collins

5

Brothers In Arms

Words & Music Mark Knopfler

Achy Breaky Heart

Words & Music by Don Von Tress

Crazy

Words & Music by Willie Nelson

Eternal Flame

Words & Music by Billy Steinberg, Tom Kelly & Susanna Hoffs

Every Little Thing She Does Is Magic

Words & Music by Sting

11

Fields Of Gold

Words & Music by Sting

Have I Told You Lately

Words & Music by Van Morrison

Hope Of Deliverance

Words & Music by Paul McCartney

I Can't Dance

Words & Music by Tony Banks, Phil Collins & Mike Rutherford

I'm Every Woman

Words & Music by Nickolas Ashford & Valerie Simpson

I Wanna Dance With Somebody
(Who Loves Me)

Words & Music by George Merrill & Shannon Rubicam

I Wonder Why

Words & Music by Curtis Stigers & Glen Ballard

Keep The Faith

Words & Music by Jon Bon Jovi, Richie Sambora & Desmond Child

Knowing Me, Knowing You

Words & Music by Benny Andersson, Stig Anderson & Bjørn Ulvaeus

More Than Words

Words & Music by Nuno Bettencourt & Gary Cherone

Moderato

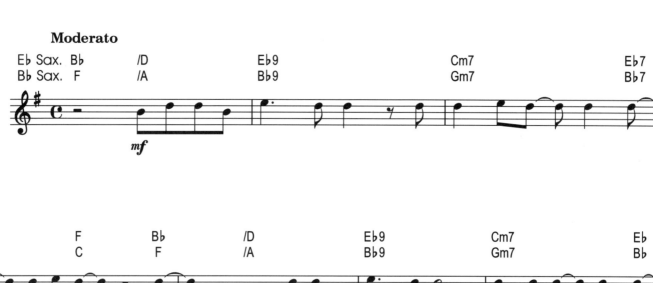

One Moment In Time

Words & Music by Albert Hammond & John Bettis

Run To You

Words & Music by Jud Friedman & Allan Rich

Super Trouper

Words & Music by Benny Andersson & Bjørn Ulvaeus

Something's Gotten Hold Of My Heart

Words & Music by Roger Cook & Roger Greenaway

Sweet Dreams Are Made Of This

Words & Music by D.A.Stewart & A.Lennox

Take A Chance On Me

Words & Music by Benny Andersson & Bjørn Ulvaeus

The Lady In Red

Words & Music by Chris De Burgh

39

Tears In Heaven

Words & Music by Eric Clapton & Will Jennings

The Way It Is

Words & Music by by B.R. Hornsby & J. Hornsby

When The Going Gets Tough

Words & Music by Wayne Brathwaite, Barry Eastmond, R.J. Lange & Billy Ocean

Why

Words & Music by Annie Lennox

Wind Of Change

Words & Music by Klaus Meine

Wonderful Life

Words & Music by Colin Vearncombe

Young At Heart

Words & Music by Robert Hodgens, Siobhan Fahey, Keren Woodward & Sarah Dallin

9/97 (28866)